Investigate Science

The Wonders of Water

by Melissa Stewart

Content Adviser: Jan Jenner, Ph.D.

Science Adviser: Terrence E. Young Jr., M.Ed.,
M.L.S., Jefferson Parish (La.) Public Schools

Reading Adviser: Rosemary G. Palmer, Ph.D.,
Department of Literacy, College of Education,
Boise State University

COMPASS POINT BOOKS MINNEAPOLIS, MINNESOTA

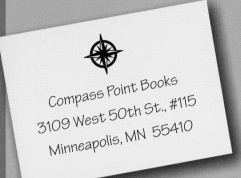

Compass Point Books
3109 West 50th St., #115
Minneapolis, MN 55410

Visit Compass Point Books on the Internet at *www.compasspointbooks.com* or e-mail your request to *custserv@compasspointbooks.com*

Photographs ©: PhotoDisc, cover, 1, 5, 8, 9, 18, 22; Creatas, 4; Kent & Donna Dannen, 6; Norbert Schaefer/Corbis, 7; Gregg Andersen, 10, 11, 12, 13, 15 (all), 21, 23 (all), 25; Corbis, 14; ASAP Ltd./Index Stock Imagery, 16; Nadia Higgins, 17 (all); Japack Company/Corbis, 19; John Mielcarek/Dembinsky Photo Assoc. Inc., 20 (all); Zefa Visual Media—Germany/Index Stock Imagery, 24.

Creative Director: Terri Foley
Managing Editor: Catherine Neitge
Editors: Nadia Higgins, Christianne C. Jones
Photo Researcher: Svetlana Zhurkina
Designer: The Design Lab
Illustrator: Jeffrey Scherer
Educational Consultant: Diane Smolinski

Library of Congress Cataloging-in-Publication Data
Stewart, Melissa.
The wonders of water / by Melissa Stewart.
   p. cm. — (Investigate science)
Summary: Introduces the characteristics and importance of water through text, illustrations, and activities.
Includes bibliographical references and index.
ISBN 0-7565-0637-9 (hardcover)
1. Water—Juvenile literature. [1. Water.] I. Title. II. Series.
   GB662.3.S74 2004
   553.7—dc22   2003022716

Note to Readers: To learn about water, scientists do experiments. They write about everything they observe. They make charts and drawings.

This book will help you study water the way a scientist does. To get started, you will need a notebook and a pencil.

In the Doing More section in the back of the book, you will find step-by-step instructions for some more fun science experiments and activities.

In this book, words that are defined in the glossary are in **bold** the first time they appear in the text.

Table of Contents

As you read this book, be on the lookout for these special symbols:

Ask an adult for help.

Turn to the back of the book for another activity.

Go to page 30 for an explanation to a question.

Water in Our Lives

Think about all the places you can find water.

Go outside and look around. Where do you see water? Water ripples in ponds and puddles. It flows out of hoses and shoots out of sprinklers. It falls from the sky.

Now search for water inside your home. Water makes a cold drink or a warm bath. It swirls in a fish tank. It flushes down the toilet. Make a list of all the places you can find water.

You couldn't live without the wonderful water all around you. What else does water do? Let's dive into some experiments and find out!

Water from sprinklers helps keep grass green.

Keep track of how much water your pet drinks.

How Much Water Do You Drink?

Did you know that two-thirds of your body is made of water? Water helps your body break down food and move your muscles. When your body needs more water, you feel thirsty.

For the next three days, write down how much water you drink. Are you surprised by the amount of water your body uses?

Do you think animals drink more or less water than people? If you have a pet, write down how much water it drinks during three days. Compare how much water you drank with how much your pet drank.

Doing More

Plants need water, too. For an experiment about plants and water, see page 26.

Did You Know?

Most people should drink about eight glasses of water every day.

Most of Earth's surface is covered with water.

How Much Water Does a Leaky Faucet Waste?

Look at a picture of Earth. Most of our planet is covered with oceans, lakes, and rivers. Only a tiny amount of Earth's water can be used for drinking, though. Ocean water is too salty. Lakes and rivers can be frozen or dirty. That's why it's important to use water wisely. See pages 27 and 28 for activities about Earth's water.

How much water can you save by fixing a leaky faucet? Turn on a faucet just a little so water slowly dribbles from it. Let the water drip into a bowl for one day. At the end of the day, pour the water into a measuring cup to find out how much you collected. Are you surprised by your results? Think about how much water a leaky faucet wastes during a whole week or month.

Doing More

What you need:
- a sink
- a large bowl
- a measuring cup

Think About It!

Do you turn off the faucet when you brush your teeth? Do you only fill the tub halfway when you take a bath? Make a list of all the ways you can save water.

Use all five senses
to examine water.

How Water Works

Observe Water in Different Containers

Look closely at a measuring cup full of water. Use all five senses—seeing, hearing, smelling, tasting, and touching—to describe the water. What color is it? Can it make any noises? How does it smell and taste? Does it feel warm or cool?

Pour the water into a tall glass, then a bowl, and then other containers in your kitchen. What shape is the water? See page 30 for an answer.

See Explanation

See page 30 for an answer.

What you need:
- a measuring cup
- water
- 4–5 clear containers, different in shape

Pour water into different containers to see how it changes shape.

11

Record Changing Water Levels

What you need:
- a sink
- 6 dinner plates
- a red bathtub crayon
- a blue bathtub crayon
- a green bathtub crayon

Plug the kitchen sink, and fill it halfway. Use a red bathtub crayon to mark the water level. Add three dinner plates, and mark the water level with a blue bathtub crayon. Add three more plates, and mark the water level with a green bathtub crayon. How does the water level change? Can you explain why? See page 30 for an explanation.

See Explanation

Add dinner plates to a sink with water to see how the water level changes.

Mark the different water levels with bathtub crayons, and compare your results.

Think About It!

You fill up the tub to take a bath. What happens to the water level in the tub once you get in? Why?

13

Think About It!

When you curl up into a ball, you sink. When you stretch out your body, you float. Why? Think about how much water is holding you up when you're curled up. Think about how much water is touching you when you stretch out. See page 30 for a full explanation.

? See Explanation

What Makes an Object Float?

Fill a large, clear bowl with water. Now look closely at a metal paper clip and a green pepper. How do they feel in your hands? Do you think the items will sink or float?

Place the metal paper clip on top of the water in the bowl. What happened? Now try the green pepper. Are you surprised by your results? Can you explain why? (Hint: As the metal paper clip sank to the bottom, it pushed water aside. Think about which weighs more—the paper clip or the amount of water it moved.) Stumped? See page 30 for an answer.

? See Explanation

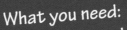
What you need:
• a large, clear bowl
• water
• a metal paper clip
• a pepper

Which item will float—a paper clip or a pepper?

Did You Know?

The Dead Sea in Israel is the saltiest body of water in the world. The water has so much salt that a person can float on top of it while reading a newspaper.

Make an Egg Float

What you need:
- a large, clear bowl
- warm water
- an egg
- salt
- a spoon for stirring

Empty the bowl, and fill it up with 6 cups of warm water. Place an egg in the water. It sinks.

Now stir 1 cup of salt into the water. Keep stirring until the water is very cloudy and you don't see any more grains of salt. That means the salt has completely **dissolved** in the water.

Put the egg in the bowl again. It floats. Can you explain why? See page 30 for an answer.

See Explanation

An egg can float in water that is salty enough.

17

Water Changing Form

Where Can You Find Ice and Steam?

At the beginning of this book, you made a list of all the places you saw water. Your list probably included the kitchen sink, but what about the freezer or the area just above a whistling tea kettle?

Amazing water is constantly changing form. The water we think about most often is a runny **liquid.** When water becomes ice, though, it is a **solid.** As steam, water is a **gas** that swirls in the air. Think about the places you can find ice and steam, and add these examples to the list of water around you.

Solid ice melts into liquid water.

When water boils, it turns into steam.

Did You Know?

Water is the only material that can be a solid, a liquid, or a gas in our everyday world.

In nature, water freezes and melts with the seasons.

What Makes Ice Melt?

When water gets cold enough, it freezes and becomes ice. What makes ice melt back into water?

Add ice cubes to two glasses that are exactly the same. Put the same number of ice cubes in each glass. Place one glass in a sunny window or under a lamp. Put the other one in a shady spot. Predict which ice cubes will melt faster. For one hour, check the glasses every 10 minutes. What makes the ice cubes in one glass melt faster than the other? See page 30 for an answer.

See Explanation

See page 30 for an answer.

What you need:
- 4–8 ice cubes
- 2 identical glasses

Add the same number of ice cubes to identical glasses.

21

What Causes Evaporation?

How do wet clothes get dry? What makes puddles disappear? When water gets warm enough, it becomes a gas. It breaks up into tiny bits that float away. This process is called **evaporation.** Look for signs of evaporation all around you.

To see evaporation in action, find two glasses that are exactly the same. Fill them with equal amounts of water, making sure that the water in both glasses is the same temperature. Place one in a warm, sunny window or under a lamp, and put one in the refrigerator. Which water will evaporate faster?

Every day for one week, compare the water levels in the two glasses. Was your guess right? Why did one glass of water evaporate faster than the other? See page 30 for an answer.

See Explanation

22

Fill two glasses with equal amounts of water.

Put one glass in the refrigerator and the other in a warm spot.

Dew comes from invisible water vapor in the air.

Did You Know?

Condensation forms the "breath" you see when you blow air out of your mouth on a cold day. It's also what makes the bathroom mirror cloud up when you take a hot shower.

Observe Condensation

Where does dew come from? The air around us is full of drops of water that are so tiny, you can't even see them. These tiny drops of water make up a gas called **water vapor.** On a chilly morning, the water vapor in the air cools down. It becomes liquid water again. This process is called **condensation.**

To see condensation in action, place an empty glass in the freezer for 10 minutes. Take the glass out, and watch what happens. Draw a picture of what you see. Can you explain what happened? See page 30 for an answer.

?
See Explanation

Now that you've thought more about water, you know how important it is to your everyday life. As you splash, flush, pour, and sip, pay attention to all the things amazing water can do.

What you need:
• a glass
• a freezer

Water vapor condenses on a chilled glass.

Doing More

What you need:
- a potato with a small hole in it
- salt
- a bowl
- plastic wrap
- a jar with a lid
- a measuring cup

Collect the Water from a Potato

On page 7, you learned that our bodies need water. So do the bodies of animals. Plants also need water. To see how much water is inside a potato, try this experiment.

Ask an Adult

1. Ask an adult to help you make a hole in a potato. The hole should be about $1/2$ inch (1.3 centimeters) wide and $1/2$ inch (1.3 centimeters) deep.

2. Fill the hole with salt and place the potato in a bowl. Cover the bowl with plastic wrap.

3. The next day, look at your experiment. All the water in the bowl came out of the potato. Pour the water into a jar with a lid.

4. Each day, repeat steps 2 and 3. Once no more water comes out, pour the water you collected into a measuring cup to find out how much water you collected. Are you surprised by how much water was in the potato?

See How Water Flows

On page 9, you learned that most of Earth's water is in lakes, rivers, and oceans. Water flows from streams and rivers into lakes and finally into oceans. To find out why, try this game.

1. Use a permanent black marker to draw a maze on a piece of heavy white paper.

2. Tape a piece of waxed paper over the white paper.

3. Lay the paper flat on a table. Carefully place a drop of water on top of the waxed paper.

4. Tip the paper back and forth to make the drop roll along the path you drew. What's the best way to make the drop go where you want it? Using this information, try to figure out why most water eventually ends up in the ocean. (Hint: Oceans are the lowest places on Earth.)

How Much of Earth's Water Can We Drink?

On page 9, you also learned that people can't drink most of the water on Earth. To find out just how little of the water we can drink, try this activity.

On page 9, you also learned

What you need:
- water
- a 1-gallon milk jug
- a measuring cup
- a permanent marker
- 2 plastic cups
- a medicine dropper
- waxed paper

1. Fill a 1-gallon (3.8-liter) milk jug with water. Pretend this is all the water on Earth.

2. Pour $1/2$ cup (120 milliliters) of the water into a measuring cup. This is all the fresh water in the world. The rest of the water in the jug stands for ocean water that's too salty to drink.

3. Use a permanent marker to write "Ocean Water" on the jug.

4. Pour $1/3$ cup (79 milliliters) of water from the measuring cup into a plastic cup. The water in the plastic cup stands for fresh water that is frozen at the North Pole and the South Pole.

5. Use a permanent marker to write "Frozen Water" on the plastic cup.

6. Pour half the water still in the measuring cup into another small plastic cup. This stands for the water that is trapped in the soil or as water vapor in the air.

7. Use a permanent marker to write "Trapped Water" on the small plastic cup.

8. The water left in the measuring cup is all the fresh water found in the world's lakes, rivers, and underground sources. Use a medicine dropper to remove five drops of that water, and place them on a piece of waxed paper. This is the water that we can drink. The rest of the water in the measuring cup is either too polluted to drink or is so far underground that we can't reach it.

Explanations to Questions

Water Changing Shape *(from page 11)*
Like all liquids, water doesn't have its own shape. It takes the shape of the container that holds it.

Plates in Water *(from page 12)*
The plates take up room in the water. Each time plates are added, they push the water higher up in the sink.

Why You Float *(from Think About It! page 14)*
When you put things in water, they push some water aside. This is called **displacement**. Different things displace different amounts of water, depending on their size, shape, and weight. When you are curled up in a ball, your body isn't touching as much water as it is when you are stretched out. When your body is in a ball, the amount of water that it displaces weighs less than you. You sink. When you are stretched out, the amount of water you displace weighs more than you. You float.

Sinking and Floating *(from page 15)*
The paper clip weighs more than the small amount of water it pushes aside, so the paper clip sinks to the bottom. The pepper weighs less than the amount of water it displaces, so the pepper floats. This experiment shows that you can't always tell whether something will float just by how much it weighs. The paper clip weighs much less than the pepper, but it sinks while the pepper floats.

Salty Water *(from page 17)*
In regular water, the amount of water that the egg displaces weighs less than the egg. The egg sinks. Adding salt makes the water heavier. In salty water, the amount of water the egg displaces weighs more than the egg. The egg floats.

Melting Ice *(from page 21)*
Heat makes ice melt. It is warmer under a lamp or by a sunny window than it is in a shady spot. The ice cubes in the warmer spot melt faster.

Evaporating Water *(from page 22)*
Heat makes water evaporate. It is warmer under a lamp or by a sunny window than it is in the refrigerator. The water in the warmer spot evaporates faster.

Condensing Water *(from page 25)*
As warm water vapor in the air hits the cold glass, the water vapor cools down. This causes the gas to condense into a liquid. The droplets of water that you see on the glass came from the air around it.

Glossary

condensation—when water vapor, which is a gas, cools down and becomes liquid water

displacement—when objects in or on water push some of the water aside

dissolve—to break up and seem to disappear in liquid

evaporation—when water gets warm enough and rises into the air as a gas

gas—a substance like air that spreads to fill any space; you can't see most gases

liquid—a substance you can pour; a liquid feels wet, can flow, and takes the shape of the container it is in

solid—a material that has its own shape and is usually hard

water vapor—water that has turned into a gas; steam is a kind of water vapor

To Find Out More

At the Library

Bailey, Jacqui. *A Drop in the Ocean: The Story of Water.* Minneapolis: Picture Window Books, 2004.

Challoner, Jack. *Wet and Dry.* Austin, Tex.: Raintree Steck-Vaughn, 1997.

Locker, Thomas. *Water Dance.* San Diego: Voyager Books/Harcourt, 2002.

Wick, Walter. *A Drop of Water: A Book of Science and Wonder.* New York: Scholastic, 1997.

On the Web

For more information on **water**, use FactHound to track down Web sites related to this book.

1. Go to *www.facthound.com*
2. Type in a search word related to this book or this book ID: 0756506379.
3. Click on the *Fetch It* button.

Your trusty FactHound will fetch the best Web sites for you!

Index

About the Author

Melissa Stewart earned a bachelor's degree in biology from Union College and a master's degree in science and environmental journalism from New York University. After editing children's science books for nearly a decade, she decided to focus on writing. She has written more than 50 science books for children and contributed articles to *ChemMatters*, *Instructor*, *MATH*, *National Geographic World*, *Natural New England*, *Odyssey*, *Ranger Rick*, *Science World*, and *Wild Outdoor World*. She also teaches writing workshops and develops hands-on science programs for schools near her home in Northborough, Massachusetts.